Profiles in American History

The Life and Times of

JOHN
ADAMS

Mitchell Lane
PUBLISHERS

P.O. Box 196 · Hockessin, Delaware 19707

Titles in the Series

The Life and Times of

JOHN
ADAMS

Jim Whiting

Mitchell Lane
PUBLISHERS

Copyright © 2007 by Mitchell Lane Publishers, Inc. All rights reserved. No part of this book may be reproduced without written permission from the publisher. Printed and bound in the United States of America.

Printing   1   2   3   4   5   6   7   8   9

Library of Congress Cataloging-in-Publication Data
Whiting, Jim, 1943–
  The life and times of John Adams/by Jim Whiting.
     p. cm. — (Profiles in American history)
  Includes bibliographical references and index.
  ISBN 1-58415-442-X (library bound: alk. paper)
     1. Adams, John, 1735–1826—Juvenile literature. 2. Presidents—United States—Biography—Juvenile literature. I. Title. II. Series.
E322.W48 2006
973.4'4'092—dc22
                                                                        2005028504
ISBN-10: 1-58415-442-X   ISBN-13: 978-1-58415-442-6

ABOUT THE AUTHOR: Jim Whiting has been a remarkably versatile and accomplished journalist, writer, editor, and photographer for more than 30 years. A voracious reader since early childhood, Mr. Whiting has written and edited about 200 non-fiction children's books. His subjects range from authors to zoologists and include contemporary pop icons and classical musicians, saints and scientists, emperors and explorers. Representative titles include *The Life and Times of Franz Liszt, The Life and Times of Julius Caesar, Charles Schulz, The Life and Times of Benjamin Franklin,* and *The Life and Times of Paul Revere.*

Other career highlights are a lengthy stint publishing *Northwest Runner,* the first piece of original fiction to appear in *Runners World* magazine, hundreds of descriptions and venue photographs for America Online, e-commerce product writing, sports editor for the *Bainbridge Island Review,* light verse in a number of magazines, and acting as the official photographer for the Antarctica Marathon.

He lives in Washington state with his wife and two teenage sons.

PHOTO CREDITS: Cover, pp. 1, 3: Library of Congress; pp. 6, 9: North Wind Picture Archives; p. 10: Picture History; p. 12: Corbis; p. 14: Library of Congress; p. 17: Corbis; p. 20: Getty Images; pp. 22, 24, 26: Library of Congress; pp. 28, 30: Getty Images; p. 32: Corbis; p. 34: Library of Congress; p. 39: Corbis

PUBLISHER'S NOTE: This story is based on the author's extensive research, which he believes to be accurate. Documentation of such research is contained on page 46.

The internet sites referenced herein were active as of the publication date. Due to the fleeting nature of some web sites, we cannot guarantee they will all be active when you are reading this book.

Contents

A celebration of the Fourth of July in the 1860s. This celebration was very similar to the ones held during Adams's lifetime. There were speeches, dancing, waving of flags, and fireworks displays.

CHAPTER
1

A Remarkable Coincidence

On July 4, 1826, Americans celebrated the fiftieth anniversary of the Declaration of Independence. They were proud of their young nation. The country had more than doubled in size. The thirteen original states had been joined by eleven more. The population had jumped from about 2.5 million colonists to more than 10 million citizens. The country was becoming more important and more respected among other nations. As a result, the events scheduled for the "Jubilee of Freedom" were especially meaningful.

As always, fireworks were popular. Many cities and towns had long parades. These often featured the men who had actually fought for freedom. Countless numbers of people stood in the hot sun in front of elevated stages decorated with red, white, and blue bunting. They listened to speakers who talked about the glory of the Revolutionary War. Many read aloud from important historical documents.

In Newport, Rhode Island, a man named John Handy read the Declaration of Independence to a crowd of his fellow citizens. Handy was standing at the same spot where he had read the same document fifty years earlier. At that time he had been a major in the Continental Army. He was the first person to bring the momentous news of independence to Newport.

Then as now, people celebrated with huge banquets that began in the early afternoon and lasted for several hours. Many kinds of meat were served. Often they were cooked in large barbecue pits. The country was still largely an agricultural society, so there were plenty of fresh fruits and vegetables. People always tried to leave a little room for pudding, pies, cakes, and, for the well-to-do, ice cream.

One of the largest banquets was in New York City. Lines of tables stretched for 500 feet. Besides food, flowers and tree branches also covered the tables. According to one news reporter, the city's mayor "took the first cut of an ox. A crowd of citizens and military then pressed forward, formed a line the whole length of the arbour, and commenced a spirited attack upon the eatables and drinkables."[1]

Two elderly men had a special interest in the occasion. Both were dying. One lay in bed in his Virginia mansion. The other was surrounded by family and friends in his modest bedroom in Quincy, Massachusetts. He may have faintly heard a speech given by Miss Caroline Whitney, who was addressing the members of the Quincy Light Infantry. The military unit was receiving a flag. It celebrated by firing off some of its cannons.

It is possible that the men were still alive because of sheer will-power. They must have wanted to be a part, however minor, of the celebrations honoring such an important anniversary. This desire stemmed from their prominent roles in creating the Declaration of Independence.

The man from Virginia was Thomas Jefferson. He had actually written the document.

The other man was John Adams. He had served with Jefferson on the five-man committee that developed the Declaration. He played a vital role in determining the final wording.

Both were among the "founding fathers" of the United States of America. The founding fathers were the handful of men most closely associated with achieving independence from Great Britain and founding the government of the new nation. Both Jefferson and Adams had been elected to the nation's highest office, the presidency.

As the nation they helped create turned fifty, Adams and Jefferson were two of the three remaining signers of the Declaration.

Delegates take turns signing the Declaration of Independence. John Hancock was the first. John Adams and Thomas Jefferson also signed it.

The other fifty-three, including Benjamin Franklin, John Hancock, and Adams's fiery cousin Samuel Adams, had long since died.

Their fellow citizens were fully aware of the importance of the two men. Starting in the early 1820s, many people traveled to see their homes. Most stood a respectful distance away. A few would press up to the doors and windows. They hoped to catch a glimpse of their heroes. According to one report, one woman even broke a window in Jefferson's mansion so that she could see him more clearly.

For this celebration, Adams had correctly predicted what would be taking place outside his window. "It will be celebrated, by succeeding Generations, as the great anniversary Festival," he wrote. "It ought to be solemnized with Pomp and Parade, with Shews [shows],

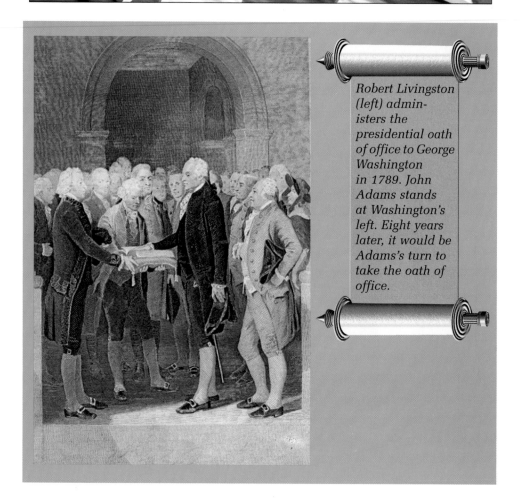

Robert Livingston (left) administers the presidential oath of office to George Washington in 1789. John Adams stands at Washington's left. Eight years later, it would be Adams's turn to take the oath of office.

Games, Sports, Guns, Bells, Bonfires and Illuminations from one End of this Continent to the other from this Time forward forever more."[2]

Adams wasn't quite as accurate in forecasting the actual date on which the celebrations would be held. On July 3, 1776, he wrote to his wife, "Yesterday the greatest Question was decided, which ever was debated in America, and a greater perhaps never was, nor will be, decided among men. A Resolution was passed without one dissenting Colony 'that these united Colonies, are, and of right ought to be, free and independent States.'"[3] He added, "The Second Day of July, 1776, will be the most memorable epocha, in the History of America."[4]

July 2 was the day on which the Second Continental Congress had finally resolved "That these United Colonies are, and of right ought to be, free and independent States, that they are absolved from all allegiance to the British Crown, and that all political connection between them and the State of Great Britain is, and ought to be, totally dissolved."[5] After the historic vote, some delegates proposed minor changes in the wording. The revised Declaration was adopted on July 4. It wasn't signed for more than a month.

The day the Declaration of Independence was adopted and the years immediately afterward were the high point of the relationship between John Adams and Thomas Jefferson. After the Revolutionary War, they drew apart in their political beliefs. In 1792, these different beliefs resulted in another historic event. The first two political parties in the United States were established. Adams helped found the Federalist Party. Jefferson played an equally important role in founding the Democratic-Republican Party.

Four years later, they became bitter rivals in the country's first real presidential election. In 1789, everyone knew that George Washington would become the country's first president. When he retired after eight years, no one had the same stature as he. The race became wide open.

Adams defeated Jefferson, opening fresh wounds in their conflict. Four years later, Jefferson reversed the outcome.

For more than a decade, the two men refused to have anything to do with each other. Then a mutual friend acted as a go-between to reunite them. With the ice broken, they exchanged letters with each other until just before their deaths. These letters have been preserved. Generations of historians and statesmen have read the letters and enjoyed the wisdom of these two remarkable men.

As night fell on July 4, 1826, millions of Americans continued the celebrations. By then, both Jefferson and Adams had died. In each other's eyes, they departed this life as equals in achievement.

For many years, history held a different opinion. Washington and Jefferson were regarded as two of this country's greatest presidents. The Washington Monument and the Jefferson Memorial in the nation's capital honor the two men. Massive side-by-side images of Washington and Jefferson inspire visitors to Mount Rushmore National Memorial in South Dakota. No one thought Adams deserved that kind of recognition.

Mount Rushmore National Monument honors four great U.S. presidents. George Washington is on the far left. The others are Thomas Jefferson (second from left), Theodore Roosevelt (second from right) and Abraham Lincoln.

In recent years, however, this line of thinking has changed. Adams has been given much more credit. He played a vital role in creating the nation. He also helped to hold it together during the crucial years immediately following its birth. In 2002, Congress passed legislation authorizing the construction of an Adams memorial in Washington, D.C.

Many historians regard the two men as they came to regard each other. They are virtually identical in their contributions to the new nation. From this point of view, nothing could be more symbolic than their deaths a few hours apart on the fiftieth anniversary of the most important date in American history.

The History of the Fourth of July

The Continental Congress passed the revised version of the Declaration of Independence on July 4. Several copies of the document were made. Riders carrying the copies fanned out from Philadelphia. They would stop in towns and villages, gather everyone together, and read the Declaration aloud. In nearly every case, the news was cause for celebration. People lit huge bonfires, shot off fireworks, rang bells, and fired their muskets into the air.

Independence Day Fireworks

Apparently no one in Congress thought of celebrating the one-year anniversary until July 3, 1777. By then, of course, it was too late to honor the day that the decision to declare independence had been made. Congress did the next best thing. They hastily put together a ceremony for July 4.

Celebrations on July 4 continued throughout the war. With the arrival of peace, the celebrations diminished in intensity and enthusiasm. In the 1790s, the rise of political parties gave a new boost to the date. One party was the Federalists, led by John Adams. They were trying to forge close economic and political ties with the British. The strong anti-British language in the Declaration was almost an embarrassment. They downplayed it.

The Democratic-Republicans, the other party, wanted to portray their leader, Thomas Jefferson, in a heroic light. They emphasized his role in creating the document. They highlighted the concept of individual rights that the Declaration stressed. The party opposed getting closer to the British. They wanted to keep the two nations separate.

Starting with Jefferson's election as president in 1800, the Democratic-Republicans soon became the dominant U.S. political party. Their heroic version of Independence Day became widely accepted. The date became increasingly popular.

In 1870, Congress declared the Fourth of July as a holiday for federal workers. Legally, that was all that Congress could do. It can't declare national holidays that apply to everyone in the country. But the Fourth of July is so important in American history that nearly every American takes the day off.

John Adams was born in a small frame house in Braintree, Massachusetts.

CHAPTER 2

Meeting Abigail

John Adams was born on October 30, 1735, in the village of Braintree, Massachusetts. He was the first child of John and Susanna Boylston Adams. Two more boys would join the family: Peter (1738) and Elihu (1741).

John Adams Sr. owned a farm near the village, which is located several miles south of Boston. He also worked as a shoemaker. He served as a deacon in his church. Susanna, like most women of the era, took care of the house and raised the children.

Young John was very active. He roamed through acres of fields and forests. He learned how to hunt and fish. His other pastimes included sailing, skating when ponds and streams froze over during the cold New England winters, flying kites, wrestling with his friends, shooting marbles, and going to dances.

John learned to read at home at an early age. Soon he went to a "dame school"— a neighbor's kitchen in which several children would assemble for instruction. Then he entered the village school. His teacher was very uninspiring. John was bored. He often played hooky. When he was about fourteen, he decided to drop out and join his father in the fields.

John Senior had other plans for his son. Much later in life, John Adams called his father "the most honestest man [I] ever knew," adding, "In wisdom, piety, benevolence and charity in proportion to

his education and sphere of his life, I have never known his superior."[1] It was very high praise, for by then, Adams had met hundreds of prominent people in both America and Europe.

Farming in New England was always uncertain. Many things could go wrong and ruin a lifetime of hard work. Like many parents, the older John Adams wanted his son to have a better life than he had. The best way of achieving that goal was through education. He was upset when his son wanted to drop out of school. Yet John Senior was wise. He knew that arguing with his son wouldn't do any good.

He pretended to go along with John. They spent a long day doing some heavy farmwork. When it was over, John Junior said that he was looking forward to another day. He probably wasn't. Then he told his father that it wasn't school he disliked, it was the teacher. His father immediately transferred him to a nearby private school. The new teacher was named Joseph Marsh. John liked him, and his studies improved dramatically. Within a year, Marsh felt that John, who was only fifteen, was ready to enter college. At that time, there was only one choice for college: Harvard. It was in Cambridge, a town a few miles from Boston and about twelve miles from Braintree.

John had to meet with the college president and some teachers. They would ask him a lot of questions. If they liked his answers, he would be admitted. John was nervous on the day of his meeting. He became even more nervous when he learned that Marsh was too ill to accompany him. He almost turned around during his ride to Cambridge. Then he realized he would be disappointing both his father and Marsh if he did. He summoned up his courage and continued. His meeting went very well, and he was admitted.

The college provided him with some financial help. His father had to pay the rest. John Senior did something that was against his principles: He sold part of his land to finance his son's education.

John was one of about twenty-five young men (there were no women there at that time) who graduated from Harvard in 1755. Nearly everyone who completed coursework at Harvard became a minister, a doctor, or a lawyer. John's father wanted his son to be a minister. John had begun keeping a journal while he was at college. He knew himself well enough to realize two things. First, he didn't have the type of personality to become a minister. He wasn't very

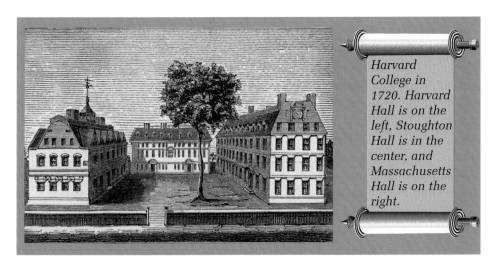

Harvard College in 1720. Harvard Hall is on the left, Stoughton Hall is in the center, and Massachusetts Hall is on the right.

tactful or warm, and his personality often rubbed people the wrong way. Second, he wanted to achieve fame. His father was disappointed with his decision, but he respected his son enough to accept it.

Adams knew what he didn't want to do, but he didn't know what he *did* want to do. He took a job as a teacher in Worcester (pronounced WUS-tur), Massachusetts. He was responsible for about a dozen students. He didn't seem to be interested in the job. One student later recalled that Adams spent much of his time staring out the window.

He felt lonely. Even though he was still a very young man, he thought of himself as washed up. "I have no books, no time, no friends. I must therefore be contented to live and die an ignorant, obscure fellow,"[2] he wrote in his journal.

Within a year, he made up his mind about his future. He decided to become a lawyer. At that time, there were no formal law schools in the colonies. Adams had to serve under a Worcester lawyer named James Putnam, who charged a fee for his help. John continued to teach so that he could pay the fee. His studies went well. He completed his studies with Putnam in 1758 and was admitted to the Massachusetts bar a year later.

His legal career didn't get off to a good start. He lost his first case. In the spring of 1761, he suffered a far greater loss. His beloved father died, the victim of an influenza epidemic that ripped through Massachusetts. John inherited a small house next to the family home

and forty acres of property. He used part of his new house to set up a law office.

Putnam had advised him to not marry early. John disregarded that advice when he began seeing Hannah Quincy. She was a member of one of Braintree's most important families. She was also a flirt and a tease. John wasn't the only young man who was interested in her. He convinced himself that she loved him. One evening he was about to propose to her. At the crucial moment, two of their friends burst unexpectedly into the room. John never had another chance to propose. Not long afterward, Hannah married someone else.

Adams owed a great deal to the two friends. If he had married Hannah, he would never have met his true soulmate.

Her name was Abigail Smith.

"His marriage to Abigail Smith was the most important decision of John Adams's life," writes historian David McCullough. "She was in all respects his equal and the part she was to play would be greater than he could possibly have imagined."[3]

They met when John was twenty-four and Abigail was fifteen. It was not a case of love at first sight. In fact, they didn't even like each other.

Soon they realized their first impressions had been wrong. John found he liked Abigail a great deal. She had read a variety of books. She was intelligent. She also had a good sense of humor.

They sent many letters back and forth, giving each other names from literature. Adams referred to Abigail as Diana (the Roman goddess of the moon) and Portia (a character from William Shakespeare's play *The Merchant of Venice*). She called him Lysander (another of Shakespeare's characters).

On October 25, 1764, they were married. Like many young newlyweds, they probably looked forward to a long and peaceful life together. They were half right. There is no doubt about the long part. Their marriage lasted for fifty-four years. Peaceful was another matter. Powerful forces far beyond their control were about to have a profound impact on their lives.

In 1760, John Adams noted in his diary: "I shall never shine, 'til some animating occasion calls forth all my powers."[4] That year, George III became King of England. It wouldn't take long for the new king to provide the "animating occasion" that Adams was hoping for. And Adams would "shine" beyond his wildest imaginings.

King George III

The future George III was born in 1738, three years after John Adams. His grandfather, George II, was king at the time. The boy's father died when George was twelve. As he got older, he believed that his grandfather hadn't been forceful enough on his subjects. This view may have come from his mother. "George, be a king,"[5] his mother had frequently urged him to do before he assumed the throne.

King George III

George III became king in 1760, at about the same time that Adams was starting to develop his law practice. Soon afterward, he married a German princess named Charlotte. They had fifteen children, more than any other British monarch.

At first, George didn't want to make the colonists angry. That changed a few years into his reign. Remembering his mother's advice, he believed that Americans should do as he ordered them to do. His policies increasingly turned the colonies against him. The Declaration of Independence singled him out for particular blame. Despite his efforts to regain control, the war dragged on. It became very expensive. Finally he had to end the war and grant independence. Despite losing the colonies, the British Empire grew substantially in other parts of the world. Trade with other nations increased.

King George presided over many significant changes in English life. When he became king, the country was still organized around agriculture. When he died in 1820, the Industrial Revolution was under way. During his reign, Great Britain united with Ireland to form the United Kingdom. George also supported the growth of the arts.

He was mentally unstable during the last years of his life. His son, the future George IV, had to assume a great deal of power.

George III's reign lasted sixty years, the second-longest in British history. Only Queen Victoria, who ruled from 1837 to 1901, spent more time on the throne.

Abigail Smith Adams as a young woman. Some people believe she was the greatest First Lady of all time. Until Barbara Bush in 2000, she was the only woman to be the wife of one president and the mother of another.

CHAPTER 3

Becoming a Patriot

For many years, France and England had been in conflict. Often their differences broke out into open war. That happened with the Seven Years' War, which was officially declared in 1756. Battles had been fought since 1754 in America, where the conflict was known as the French and Indian War.

The war ended in 1763, the year before Abigail and John Adams were married. The British won. The war had been very expensive. Some people in the British government, including the king, believed that the colonies should be taxed to help pay for it.

The colonists used paper for many purposes, such as for newspapers and legal documents. Parliament passed the Stamp Act in 1765, which said that the colonists had to buy a stamp and put it on all types of papers. The colonists were angry about this tax. Mobs beat up the men who tried to sell the stamps.

Adams was just as angry, but he didn't believe in violence. His protest took a different form. He said the Stamp Act was illegal. He wanted to use existing laws to fight the tax, believing that the best way to make changes was through the justice system.

That year was important to Adams in another way. His first child, Abigail, was born. She was nicknamed Nabby. Three sons—John Quincy (1767), Charles (1770), and Thomas (1772)—would follow.

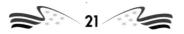

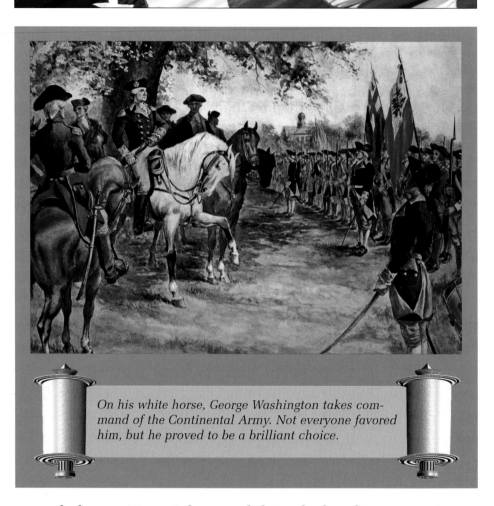

On his white horse, George Washington takes command of the Continental Army. Not everyone favored him, but he proved to be a brilliant choice.

wanted the position. Other candidates had military experience. Although Washington had never commanded an army, Adams knew that choosing Washington would help unify the colonies. Adams had made the perfect choice for his wife. Washington proved a perfect choice for commander. On several occasions, Washington's determination was the only thing that enabled the Continental Army to survive. If not for him, the Revolution may have collapsed.

After the initial excitement that Lexington and Concord had generated, many Patriots became discouraged. It seemed as if the war would continue for a long time. Support for independence began to decline. Early in 1776, this support suddenly and dramatically increased. The rallying cry came from a very unlikely source.

The Boston Massacre

The landing of British troops in Boston in September 1768 created more friction in the colonies. Boston citizens didn't want the soldiers there. They called the troops "Redcoats" because of their scarlet coats. They also called them "lobster backs" because the soldiers reminded them of the bright red shells of cooked lobsters. Both terms were insults. Even young children taunted the soldiers.

A man dressed as a colonial British soldier

The British yelled back. They called the people "cowardly rascals." The soldiers were angry and frustrated. They were under strict orders not to fire their muskets. Fistfights between the two sides were common.

On March 5, 1770, a British soldier, standing by himself, got into an argument with a teenager. He struck the boy. A crowd gathered, with many people throwing snowballs and chunks of ice at the soldier. He called for help.

An officer and seven soldiers answered his call. By this time several hundred people had joined the crowd. They pressed tightly around the handful of soldiers. One of the biggest men pushed a soldier and knocked him down. The soldier, enraged, fired his musket into the crowd. The other soldiers did the same thing. Five Boston citizens were killed.

The British soldiers were arrested and charged with murder. Meanwhile, Patriot leaders such as Samuel Adams and Paul Revere wanted to make it seem that the British were completely to blame. Adams immediately branded the incident the "Boston Massacre." Revere made an engraving of the event that didn't show the circumstances very accurately.

Revere made it seem as if the officer had ordered his men to fire their muskets. That wasn't true. He put smiles on the faces of some of the soldiers. It appeared that they were enjoying the killing. By contrast, the people of Boston appeared harmless and peaceful.

The engraving was circulated throughout the American colonies. It inspired a great deal of outrage. Even today, it is one of the most famous pictures about the Revolutionary era. As historian David Hackett Fischer notes, "The print helped to create an image of British tyranny and American innocence that still shapes our memory of the event."[1]

This image of John Adams was probably made about the time the Revolutionary War started. Adams was among the leaders of the movement toward independence. One of his most important contributions was proposing George Washington as commander in chief.

CHAPTER 4

The Birth of a Nation

Late in 1774, an almost penniless immigrant arrived in Philadelphia from England. His name was Thomas Paine. Just over a year after his arrival, he wrote a pamphlet called *Common Sense.* It was one of the most important political documents ever published in America. Paine became an overnight celebrity.

Common Sense made its readers want independence. The Continental Congress knew the colonies by themselves probably couldn't stand up to the British. They needed more money, more men, and more of many other things. To get those things, they would have to make an alliance with a foreign country. France was the obvious choice. The French had fought the English before. However, the French refused to help. They didn't want to do anything that would upset the British and cause still another war.

Congress made a brave decision. They would declare that they were independent. As an independent nation, they would have a better chance of getting support from other nations. Many people thought that Adams should write the Declaration of Independence because he was a lawyer, and the Declaration would be a legal document. Adams knew that writing it would be a great honor. He suggested that Jefferson write it instead. He explained his thinking in a letter to Jefferson: "Reason first, you are a Virginian, and a Virginian

The committee that drew up the Declaration of Independence. From left, Benjamin Franklin, Thomas Jefferson, John Adams, Robert Livingston, and Roger Sherman. Jefferson did most of the actual writing.

ought to appear at the head of this business. Reason second, I am obnoxious, suspected, unpopular. You are very much otherwise. Reason third, you can write ten times better than I can."[1]

The first reason was probably the most important. Even though the war had started in New England, the unity of the colonies was very fragile. Many other colonists, especially those in the South, deeply distrusted the ones in New England. Adams knew it was important for someone outside of New England to write this important document.

Several of the colonies weren't sure that they even wanted to declare independence. Congress had voted in favor of it, but some

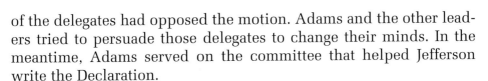

of the delegates had opposed the motion. Adams and the other leaders tried to persuade those delegates to change their minds. In the meantime, Adams served on the committee that helped Jefferson write the Declaration.

Adams was under a lot of pressure. Being away from Abigail and the rest of his family only increased his stress. It helped that he had completely trusted Abigail to take care of the farm while he was gone. It also helped that the two of them wrote many letters to each other. He felt comfortable enough with her to reveal his innermost thoughts, and the feeling was mutual. Abigail fully supported him in the work he was doing. She wasn't afraid to make suggestions. Some of her suggestions would be considered unusual for that era.

"In the new Code of Laws which I suppose it will be necessary for you to make I desire you would Remember the Ladies," she wrote. "Do not put such unlimited power into the hands of the Husbands. Remember all Men would be tyrants if they could. . . . Give up the harsh title of Master for the more tender and endearing one of Friend."[2]

"I cannot but laugh,"[3] he replied. John Adams, like most men of his era, thought her ideas about women's rights were too far ahead of the times.

The ideas that his committee was putting forth were also ahead of the times. When Congress voted on the Declaration on July 1, only nine colonies were in favor. They included the New England states (Massachusetts, New Hampshire, Connecticut, Rhode Island), New Jersey, Maryland, Virginia, North Carolina, and Georgia. South Carolina and Pennsylvania voted no. Delaware had only two delegates, and they couldn't agree. New York's delegates didn't cast any votes. Their instructions wouldn't allow them to approve anything that would separate their colony from the British.

Congress decided to vote again the next day. South Carolina and Pennsylvania changed their minds. Delaware's third delegate, Caesar Rodney, arrived. He broke his colony's tie by favoring independence. Now the vote was 12-0. Again New York didn't vote. When New York finally voted on July 9, the decision became unanimous.

It was one thing to declare independence. It was far more difficult to actually establish it. Washington suffered a disastrous military defeat in New York soon afterward. His army barely managed to

A street scene in Paris from the era that Benjamin Franklin lived there. Aristocrats stroll while a group of less privileged women does laundry. It was Franklin's genius that he got along with all levels of French society.

escape. Other defeats followed. Washington, making a desperate gamble, led a daring Christmas Day raid on the Hessian army at Trenton. The Hessians were German troops that the British had hired to help them. The raid was successful and gave the colonists some hope. An even more important victory came the following October. American troops captured an entire British army under General John Burgoyne at the Battle of Saratoga. Now the Americans appeared to have a chance at victory. The French offered an alliance.

Benjamin Franklin handled the American delegation in Paris to ask for the alliance with France. In 1778, Congress asked Adams to

join Franklin and offer his assistance. Adams decided the crossing was too dangerous for Abigail to accompany him. Instead he took his ten-year-old son, John Quincy. He was right about the dangers. A cannonball fired by a British ship nearly ripped his head off early in the voyage.

Adams took a dislike to Franklin. Some historians believe that he might have been jealous of the older man. Franklin had been world famous for nearly a quarter century, ever since his groundbreaking experiments with electricity. Compared to Franklin, Adams was a nobody. Further dampening his reception, some of the French had been expecting his famous cousin Samuel. Getting John instead was a letdown.

One result was that he had very little to do. Frustrated, he returned home less than a year later.

He didn't have much time to rest. Massachusetts decided to draw up a state constitution. Adams wrote most of the document.

Not long afterward, Adams was asked to return to France. The Revolution had dragged on for a long time. The British were finally considering peace. Adams sailed again, this time with both John Quincy and Charles.

Once again he was frustrated. The French wanted to lead the talks. In addition, the tide of war had turned against the Americans. The British, sensing they were about to win, were no longer interested in negotiating.

Adams and the boys went to Holland. He was more successful there. Holland agreed to formally recognize the United States as an independent nation. Adams was also able to arrange for a substantial loan. Then John Quincy received an attractive offer. The American minister to Russia asked the boy to join him and serve as his secretary. Charles, lonely without his brother, sailed home.

Early in 1782, Adams received electrifying news. With French support, Washington had won the Battle of Yorktown in October 1781. The British decided it would be too expensive to continue the fight. They wanted peace. This time they didn't back out.

Adams returned to Paris. He joined Franklin and John Jay in lengthy negotiations with the British. The peace treaty was signed in September 1783.

John Quincy Adams in his late twenties. By then he had already begun an important political career. He became the sixth president of the United States in 1825.

Adams stayed in Europe. A year later, he learned that he would become the first U.S. ambassador to Great Britain. He asked Abigail, Nabby, and the boys to join him. The family became close friends with Thomas Jefferson, who had been appointed as ambassador to France.

Once again, Adams soon became frustrated. Hardly anyone in England paid attention to him. The one bright spot was the marriage of Nabby to Adams's secretary, Colonel William Smith.

The Constitutional Convention convened in Philadelphia in 1787. Adams was still in Europe. He had written *A Defense of the Constitutions of Government of the United States.* The book appeared just before the convention, and the delegates respected the ideas he expressed in it. Many of his ideas were incorporated into the U.S. Constitution.

In 1788, Adams decided to come home. He had been overseas almost constantly for a decade. He thought that his days of public service were over.

He was wrong.

Common Sense

The situation for the Patriots looked grim as 1776 began. Many American troops around Boston had gone home at the end of 1775. Their terms of enlistment had expired. Most colonists still wanted to work out a settlement with England.

That attitude changed within a few weeks. It was caused by a pamphlet called *Common Sense.* Its

Thomas Paine

author, Thomas Paine, attacked the widespread belief that King George III cared for the colonists. His words were shocking for their boldness.

Paine also laid out reasons for the colonies to declare independence. "I offer nothing more than simple facts, plain arguments and common sense."[4] He wrote down a series of step-by-step arguments. Readers could easily follow them.

The pamphlet created a sensation. A remarkable half million copies were printed. There were only about two and a half million people in the colonies.

Before *Common Sense* was published, it seemed as if a few Patriot leaders were trying to pull the rest of the people along with them. Now the situation was reversed. The people were pushing their leaders toward independence. Adams wrote later, "'Common Sense' is the most brilliant pamphlet written during the American Revolution, and one of the most brilliant pamphlets ever written in the English language."[5]

Thomas Paine was an unlikely hero. He was born in England in 1737. He worked at a number of jobs, but failed in every one. The only thing he was good at was talking.

He sailed to America late in 1774 and quickly fell in love with his adopted country. The news of Lexington and Concord shocked him. Convinced that the colonies should separate from England, he wrote *Common Sense.* He wrote other pamphlets after the war began that provided encouragement during the difficult times.

When the war ended, he went back to Europe. He was nearly guillotined during the French Revolution. He returned to the United States in 1802 and died, virtually forgotten, seven years later.

For Your Information

John Adams experienced many problems during his term as president. People unfairly compared him with George Washington. He had some solid accomplishments. One was his appointment of John Marshall as Chief Justice of the Supreme Court. Many historians consider Marshall the greatest man to hold the position.

CHAPTER 5

Mr. President

To his astonishment, Adams received a hero's welcome when he arrived in Boston. While still in London, he had purchased an eighty-three-acre property called Peacefield. It was only about a mile from his old home in Braintree. John and Abigail believed that the estate would live up to its name. Adams thought he would resume his legal practice. It would generate enough income to support his family. Then they could finally retire.

His country had other ideas for him. The Constitution had just been adopted. It called for a president and vice president. There was no doubt that the first president would be George Washington. People were already referring to him as the Father of His Country.

At that time, every elector cast two votes. The person who received the most votes would be president, and the one with the second most votes would be vice president. Every one of the 69 electors gave Washington one of their votes. John Adams was the runner-up with 34 votes. He was far ahead of John Jay, who received 9 votes. Nine other candidates shared the remaining 26 votes.

Washington and Adams began serving their terms in New York City, the temporary capital. Then they moved to Philadelphia.

Adams soon realized that his office had little power. If Washington died, he would become president. Adams also presided over the

U.S. Senate. In the event of tie votes, he would cast the deciding vote. Other than that, there was little for him to do.

Adams had always been outspoken. He participated eagerly in Senate debates. Soon the Senate was fed up. It passed a resolution that forbade him to speak anymore. He was forced to listen hour after hour to speeches by men whom he often didn't respect.

Even worse, Washington didn't consider Adams to be a member of his executive cabinet. He felt that his duties in the Senate made him a member of the legislative branch. When Congress wasn't in session, Adams would go home.

His only consolation was his tie-breaking votes. Several came in support of a very important compromise. The differences between Northern and Southern states continued. The Northern states wanted the federal government to pay their war debts. The South wanted the new capital to be built in one of their states. Alexander Hamilton and Thomas Jefferson worked out a compromise. The South agreed to pay the war debts. In return, the North agreed to support a capital on land donated by Virginia and Maryland. The land was named the District of Columbia, and at first the capital was called Federal City. Within a year it was renamed Washington.

Despite the lack of satisfaction that his office provided, Adams ran again in 1792. Washington received all 132 votes. Adams had 77, while the runner-up, George Clinton of New York, had 50. Thomas Jefferson was next in line, with 4.

By this time, the nation had formed two political parties. Washington and Adams were Federalists, and Clinton and Jefferson were Democratic-Republicans. Federalists emphasized the power of the central government. The Democratic-Republicans wanted the states to have more power.

Adams disliked political parties. He thought they were too divisive. Many other men said the same thing—in public. In private, they often did things that would help their party even if it hurt the nation as a whole. John Adams was different. "Adams was the most undependable party man in the country," says historian Richard Brookhiser. "Only Adams remained true to his professed beliefs."[1]

Adams and Jefferson realized that they had very different views on important issues. One of the most important was the French Revolution, which had broken out in 1789. Even though it had been

inspired by the American Revolution, it took a very different course. Many people were sent to the guillotine. Jefferson approved of the increasing power of the French people. Adams was horrified at what the people were doing with their power.

Washington decided not to seek a third term in 1796. For the first time, there would be a real presidential election. As the vice president, Adams was the natural choice of the Federalists. Jefferson ran as the candidate of the Democratic-Republican Party.

Jefferson owned vast tracts of land and scores of slaves, yet he presented himself as the champion of the common man. In contrast, Adams was the son of a common man, yet his enemies portrayed him as the leader of the elite.

The candidates stood apart from the actual campaigning. They gave that task to their subordinates. The election took on a nasty edge. Each side said horrible things about the other.

In a very close election, Adams emerged victorious. He had 71 electoral votes; Jefferson, 68; and Thomas Pinckney, 59.

John Adams was inaugurated in March 1797. One of his first acts was to meet with Jefferson. He asked his rival—now his vice president—to join him in trying to govern the country without regard to party politics. Jefferson refused.

Almost immediately Adams had to deal with a difficult international situation. Britain and France had gone to war again in 1793. Both navies were capturing American merchant ships to make sure that their cargoes wouldn't aid the other side. Many American merchants were going broke.

The Federalists wanted war with France. The Democratic-Republicans supported a war with England. Adams, knowing that the United Sates was still very weak militarily, wanted a diplomatic solution instead. He sent three commissioners to France. Three Frenchmen met the commissioners. The men said the only way the meeting would take place was if the United States paid a bribe. Adams did not keep the bribery demand a secret. People in the United States were outraged when they learned of the incident. It became known as the XYZ Affair.

Adams knew a strong navy was important. He used the plight of the merchant ships to urge Congress to appropriate funds for build-

ing naval ships. Congress was convinced. The agreement gave Adams probably his greatest wave of popularity during his presidency.

War fever began to rise. Many Americans became concerned with internal security. Congress passed the Alien and Sedition Acts. The Alien Acts included laws aimed at people who hadn't been born in the United States. They raised suspicions against newly arrived immigrants. The President could even deport immigrants if he suspected them of illegal acts. The Sedition Act made it illegal to assemble to protest government policies. It outlawed newspapers from publishing negative opinions, clearly violating the Bill of Rights.

Adams signed the bills. There was a strong public outcry against them. The opposition grew stronger when several newspaper editors were arrested. One of them was Benjamin Franklin's grandson.

Troubles with France came to a head the following year. The French appeared more open to negotiation. That was fine with Adams. He appointed a Democratic-Republican to lead the American team, which outraged some of his fellow Federalists. The negotiations were successful, ending the threat of war.

Alexander Hamilton had been Treasury Secretary under Washington. Even though he was a Federalist, he didn't like Adams. He actively worked against him, which only served to benefit Jefferson. Many people already favored Jefferson because he had opposed many of Adams's policies.

Adams and Jefferson were the two main candidates in the 1800 election. Jefferson felt that New York was the key to his campaign. He persuaded Aaron Burr of New York to run with him. Burr had received 30 votes in the previous election. He would be a strong candidate.

The election was even more bitter than the one in 1796. One newspaper warned that awful things would happen if Jefferson became president. "Murder, robbery . . . will be openly taught and practiced . . . the soil will be soaked with blood, and the nation black with crimes,"[2] it claimed. Others accused Jefferson of being non-Christian—a serious charge in a country that had been founded primarily by Christians.

For Adams, Hamilton's attacks were damaging enough. Even worse were the assaults from his opponents, who spread a false

story about him. According to the story, Adams would overturn the Constitution, then he would establish a hereditary monarchy. According to this "plan," one of his sons would marry a daughter of King George III.

The results were a straight party-line vote. The Democratic-Republicans, Jefferson and Burr, each had 73 votes. Adams had 65; Pinckney, 64; and fellow Federalist John Jay, 1. The electors had intended that Jefferson be president and Burr his vice president, but the system then in effect didn't spell out any way of breaking a tie vote.

Congress voted dozens of times, but they couldn't break the tie. Finally Hamilton persuaded a few Federalists who had supported Burr to turn in blank ballots. That gave the election to Jefferson. Burr was enraged. He killed Hamilton in 1804 in one of the nation's most famous duels.

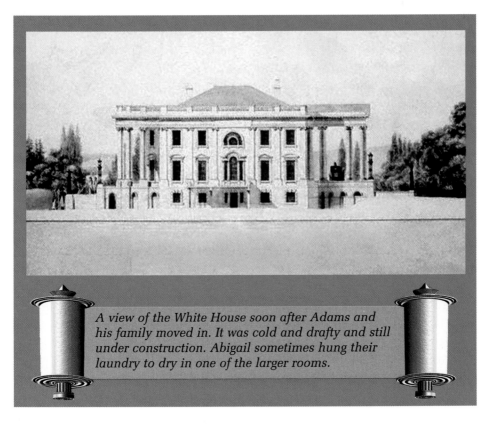

A view of the White House soon after Adams and his family moved in. It was cold and drafty and still under construction. Abigail sometimes hung their laundry to dry in one of the larger rooms.

Near the end of his term, Adams became the first president to live in the White House. The building, which was was still under construction, was dark and drafty. He also appointed a number of judges. Many people disapproved of this action because it came after he had lost the election but before Jefferson took office. Especially significant was the appointment of John Marshall as Chief Justice of the U.S. Supreme Court. Many historians believe that Marshall was the country's best Chief Justice.

Adams left the White House and returned to his home in what was now Quincy. He was out of the public eye for the first time in more than twenty-five years. It was a difficult period. He had to deal with the pain of rejection. Many people appeared to have forgotten him—among them, the new president. Adams wrote a generous letter to Jefferson, wishing him well. Jefferson never responded.

He had other problems. He wasn't a wealthy man. Some of his investments failed. Things were difficult with his family. Though he and Abigail remained as close as ever, Charles, an alcoholic, had died shortly before the 1800 election. In 1803, Thomas settled nearby. He too was an alcoholic.

On the other hand, John Quincy was becoming more and more successful. He decided to run for Congress. It was the beginning of a distinguished political career that culminated in 1824. John Quincy Adams was elected to be the nation's sixth president. Until 2000, with the election of George W. Bush, it would be the only time that a son would follow his father into the White House.

John Adams's bitterness with Jefferson continued for more than a decade after the election. They had a mutual friend named Benjamin Rush, who had also signed the Declaration of Independence. Rush told them that he had had a dream. In the dream, Adams and Jefferson had been friends again. Adams wrote a friendly letter to Jefferson on January 1, 1812. The timing makes it seem as if it were a New Year's resolution. Jefferson replied. The two men began exchanging letters regularly. They wrote about what was going on in their lives, their opinions, and reconciliations of their political differences.

Abigail died in 1818. Adams was devastated. With Abigail gone, his health grew worse. Meanwhile, so did Jefferson's.

Adams sent the final letter of the long correspondence with Jefferson on April 17, 1826. Two months later, Jefferson turned

down an invitation to become a public part of the fiftieth anniversary of the signing of the Declaration of Independence. Instead he sent a letter, which concluded: "Let the annual return to this day forever refresh our recollections of these rights [as set forth in the Declaration of Independence], and an undiminished devotion to them."[3] It would be his last bit of advice to the nation he had served so well for so long.

At the same time, a delegation visited Adams in his home. They wanted to know if he had any words to deliver to the people at the upcoming celebration. "Independence forever!"[4] he replied.

Early on the morning of the Fourth, it became apparent that Adams was failing rapidly. He was breathing with great difficulty.

Jefferson had fallen unconscious on July 2. He awoke briefly the following evening but soon relapsed. He awoke again early on the morning of the Fourth. He said a few final words to his servants and became unconscious again. He died at about one in the afternoon.

Adams lived about five hours longer. The people at his bedside said there had been a late afternoon thunderstorm. As he died, there was a clap of thunder. Then a strong beam of sunshine poked through the clouds and entered the bedroom.

It was a stunning coincidence that two men so closely associated with the Declaration of Independence would die on its fiftieth anniversary. Many people saw it as evidence that God approved of the United States. John Quincy Adams wrote: "The time, the manner, the coincidence . . . are visible and palpable marks of Divine favor."[5] Daniel Webster was one of the nation's most famous public speakers. He said that the two men dying on such an important occasion provided absolute proof "that our country, and his benefactors, are objects of [God's] care."[6]

Writing nearly two hundred years later, author and TV anchorman Tom Brokaw would identify the men and women who came of age during World War II and fought the world's widest-ranging conflict as the "Greatest Generation." Adams might have disagreed. In one of his letters to Jefferson, he wrote that the generation living at end of the eighteenth century was "the most honorable"[7] to human nature.

It is hard to find any American who was more honorable than John Adams.

John Quincy Adams

President George W. Bush is the son of another president, George H. W. Bush. But he isn't the first son to follow his father into the White House. That honor goes to John Quincy Adams.

Born in 1767, John Quincy Adams spent nearly his entire life in politics. In 1775 he was old enough to watch, from the top of a hill near his home in Braintree, Massachusetts, the famous Battle of Bunker Hill. His father took him to Europe several

John Quincy Adams

times on diplomatic missions. While he was there, he was invited to go to Russia as the secretary of the American minister. After the war, he attended Harvard College and became a lawyer. At the age of twenty-six, he began a diplomatic career. In 1802 he was elected to the U.S. Senate. Six years later President James Madison appointed him as minister to Russia. He served as secretary of state for President James Monroe.

In 1824, he ran for president against three other men. Andrew Jackson won the popular vote, but he didn't have enough electoral votes. Henry Clay, another candidate, gave his support to Adams, which gave Adams enough electoral votes to win the presidency. Jackson was furious and vowed to get revenge. He defeated Adams in 1828 and became president.

Adams's defeat wasn't the end of his political career. In 1830, he was appointed a member of the House of Representatives. He served there with distinction for the rest of his life.

Like his father, he always remained true to his principles. In 1841, he defended the slaves who had overpowered the crew on the slave ship *Amistad.* The case involved the question of whether the slaves should be sent in chains to Cuba or set free. Adams hesitated to take the case. He felt he was out of practice in trying court cases. He was still good enough to win.

Another example of his integrity came in 1848. The House was debating a resolution to award medals to several generals in the Mexican-American War. Adams had opposed the war. He argued against the resolution. Moments after he finished, he collapsed. He died that night.

Chapter Notes

Chapter 1
A Remarkable Coincidence

1. James Heintze, "Fourth of July Dinners Prior to the Civil War," quoting *Richmond Enquirer,* July 14, 1826, p. 4; online at http://gurukul. american.edu/heintze/dinner.htm

2. John Rhodehamel (editor), *The American Revolution: Writings from the War of Independence* (New York: The Library of America, 2001), p. 127.

3. Ibid., p. 125.

4. Ibid., p. 127.

5. Pauline Maier, "Making Sense of the Fourth of July," http://usinfo. state.gov/usa/infousa/facts/symbols/ sense.htm

Chapter 2
Meeting Abigail

1. David McCullough, *John Adams* (New York: Simon and Schuster, 2001), p. 33.

2. Ibid., p. 41.

3. Ibid., p. 57.

4. Ibid., p. 47.

5. Jack Shepherd, *The Adams Chronicles* (Boston: Little Brown and Company, 1975), p. 22.

Chapter 3
Becoming a Patriot

1. David Hackett Fischer, *Paul Revere's Ride* (New York: Oxford University Press, 1994), p. 23.

Chapter 4
The Birth of a Nation

1. William H. Hallahan, *The Day the American Revolution Began: 19 April 1775* (New York: William Morrow, 2000), p. 72.

2. John Rhodehamel (editor), *The American Revolution: Writings from the War of Independence* (New York: The Library of America, 2001), p. 117.

3. John Ferling, *John Adams: A Life* (New York: Henry Holt, 1992), p. 172.

4. Hallahan, p. 159.

5. Ibid.

Chapter 5
Mr. President

1. Richard Brookhiser, *America's First Dynasty: The Adamses, 1735–1918* (New York: The Free Press, 2002), p, 47.

2. Willard Sterne Randall, *Thomas Jefferson: A Life* (New York: Henry Holt, 1993), p. 543.

3. David McCullough, *John Adams* (New York: Simon and Schuster, 2001), p. 650.

4. Jack Shepherd, *The Adams Chronicles* (Boston: Little Brown and Company, 1975), p. 295.

5. Ibid.

6. McCullough, p. 648.

7. Ibid., p. 650.

Chronology

1735	Is born on October 30 in Braintree, Massachusetts
1751	Enters Harvard College
1755	Graduates from Harvard College; begins teaching school
1759	Is admitted to the Massachusetts bar
1761	Father dies
1764	Marries Abigail Smith
1765	Daughter Abigail (Nabby) is born; he becomes politically active following the passage of the Stamp Act by the British Parliament
1767	Son John Quincy is born
1770	Son Charles is born; is attorney for British soldiers accused of murder in the Boston Massacre
1772	Son Thomas is born
1774	Is a member of the Continental Congress, serving on many committees
1776	Helps draft the Declaration of Independence and signs it
1778	Sails to Europe with son John Quincy
1779	Draws up Massachusetts State Constitution
1782	Becomes first U.S. ambassador to The Netherlands (to 1788)
1783	Negotiates and signs peace treaty ending the Revolutionary War
1785	Becomes first U.S. ambassador to Great Britain (to 1788)
1789	Is elected vice president of the United States
1796	Is elected the second president of the United States
1800	Is defeated by Thomas Jefferson in his bid for reelection
1812	Reconciles with Jefferson
1818	Wife, Abigail, dies
1824	Son John Quincy wins election as the sixth president of the United States
1826	Dies on July 4
2002	Congress authorizes the construction of an Adams memorial in Washington, D.C.

Timeline in History

1630	Boston, Massachusetts, is founded.
1732	George Washington is born.
1743	Thomas Jefferson is born.
1754	The French and Indian War begins in North America.
1760	George III becomes King of England; his reign lasts until his death in 1820, the second-longest in British history.
1775	The Revolutionary War begins on April 19 with the Battles of Lexington and Concord.
1776	The Declaration of Independence is adopted on July 4.
1789	With the adoption of the U.S. Constitution, George Washington becomes the first president of the United States. The French Revolution begins with the storming of the Bastille, the notorious prison in Paris.
1792	The village of Braintree becomes part of Quincy, Massachusetts.
1799	George Washington dies.
1809	Future president Abraham Lincoln is born.
1826	Thomas Jefferson dies on July 4.
1828	John Quincy Adams loses presidential election to Andrew Jackson.
1832	Charles Carroll of Carrollton, Maryland, the last surviving signer of the Declaration of Independence, dies.
1848	John Quincy Adams dies.
1865	Abraham Lincoln is assassinated a few days after the Civil War ends.
1885	The Washington Monument is dedicated.
1943	The Jefferson Memorial is dedicated.
1988	George H. W. Bush is elected president.
2000	George W. Bush is elected president.
2005	U.S. spacecraft Deep Impact intentionally collides with a comet on July 4 for the largest Fourth of July blast in history.

Further Reading

For Young Adults

Adkins, Jan. *John Adams: Young Revolutionary.* New York: Aladdin Paperbacks, 2002.

Benge, Janet, and Geoff Benge. *John Adams: Independence Forever.* Seattle: YWAM Publishing, 2002.

Feinberg, Barbara Silberdick. *John Adams.* New York: Children's Press, 2003.

Harness, Cheryl. *The Revolutionary John Adams.* Washington, D.C.: National Geographic Society, 2003.

St. George, Judith. *John and Abigail Adams: An American Love Story.* New York: Holiday House, 2001.

Wagoner, Jean Brown. *Abigail Adams: Girl of Colonial Days.* New York: Aladdin Paperbacks, 1992.

Works Consulted

Brookhiser, Richard. *America's First Dynasty: The Adamses, 1735–1918.* New York: The Free Press, 2002.

Ellis, Joseph J. *Passionate Sage: The Character and Legacy of John Adams.* New York: W. W. Norton, 1993.

Ferling, John. *John Adams: A Life.* New York: Henry Holt, 1992.

Fischer, David Hackett. *Paul Revere's Ride.* New York: Oxford University Press, 1994.

Hallahan, William H. *The Day the American Revolution Began: 19 April 1775.* New York: William Morrow, 2000.

McCullough, David. *John Adams.* New York: Simon and Schuster, 2001.

Rhodehamel, John (editor). *The American Revolution: Writings from the War of Independence.* New York: The Library of America, 2001.

Shepherd, Jack. *The Adams Chronicles.* Boston: Little Brown and Company, 1975.

On the Internet

Colonial Hall: "Biography of John Adams"
http://www.colonialhall.com/adamsj/adamsj.asp

Biography of John Quincy Adams
http://www.whitehouse.gov/history/presidents/ja6.html

Heintze, James. "Fourth of July Dinners Prior to the Civil War"
http://gurukul.american.edu/heintze/dinner.htm

Heintze, James R. "Fourth of July Celebrations Database"
http://www.american.edu/heintze/fourth.htm

Maier, Pauline. "Making Sense of the Fourth of July"
http://usinfo.state.gov/usa/infousa/facts/symbols/sense.htm

Signers of the Declaration of Independence
http://www.ushistory.org/declaration/signers/

Thomas Paine
http://www.ushistory.org/paine

Glossary

arbour (AR-bur) (also spelled arbor)
a sheltered area, most often formed by vines growing over supports.

bunting (BUN-ting)
fabric used for decoration, usually in the colors of a national flag.

epocha (EH-puh-kuh)
different spelling of *epoch,* which is any significant period in history.

guillotine (GEE-yah-teen)
a device with a heavy blade suspended between two tracks, at the bottom of which lies a person condemned to death; when the blade is released, it cuts off the person's head.

hereditary (heh-REH-dih-tay-ree)
passing directly from one generation to the next.

hooky (HUH-kee)
the unexcused skipping of school in order to amuse oneself.

militiamen (muh-LIH-shuh-men)
armed citizens who have some military training but are not members of a regular army.

repealed (ree-PEELD)
canceled a law that had been enacted.

Index